Business English Phrases

By

Grenville Kleiser

A request for further particulars will not involve any obligation

A telegram is enclosed for your use, as this matter is urgent

Accept our thanks for your recent remittance

Acknowledging the receipt of your recent inquiry

After examination we can confidently say

After very carefully considering

Again thanking you for the inquiry

Agreeable to our conversation

An addressed envelope is enclosed for your convenience

An early reply will greatly oblige

Answering your recent inquiry

Any information you may give us will be appreciated

Any time that may suit your convenience

As a matter of convenience and economy

As a special favor we ask

As directed in your letter, we are shipping to you

As explained in our previous letter

As it will give us an opportunity to demonstrate our ability

As stated in our previous letter

As we have received no response from you

As you, doubtless, are aware

As you probably have been told

As your experience has probably shown you

Assuring you of every courtesy

Assuring you of our entire willingness to comply with your request

Assuring you of prompt and careful cooperation

At the present writing

At the suggestion of one of our patrons

At your earliest opportunity

Awaiting the favor of your prompt attention

Awaiting the pleasure of serving you

Awaiting your early communication

Awaiting your further commands

Awaiting your pleasure

Believing you will answer this promptly

Complying with your request

Conditions make it obligatory for us

D

Do not hesitate to let us know

Do not overlook this opportunity

Do you realize that you can

Enclosed please find a memorandum

Enclosed we beg to hand you

Enclosed you will find a circular which will fully explain

For some years past

For your convenience we enclose a stamped envelope

For your further information we take pleasure in sending to you

Frankly, we believe it is extremely worthwhile for you

From the standpoint of serviceability

Here is a complete answer to

Here is your opportunity

Hoping for a continuance of your interest

Hoping for a definite reply

Hoping that our relations may prove mutually satisfactory

Hoping to be favored with your order

How may we serve you further?

However, because of the special circumstances attached

I am compelled to inform you

I am confident that you will be thoroughly satisfied

I am directed to say to you

I am, gentlemen, yours faithfully

I am giving the matter my personal attention

I am, my dear sir, yours faithfully

I am still holding this offer open to you

I ask that you be good enough

I beg to request that you give me some information

I believe I understand perfectly just how you feel about

I have been favorably impressed by your

I have now much pleasure in confirming

I have pleasure in acknowledging

I have the honor to acknowledge the receipt

I have the honor to remain

I herewith submit my application

I highly appreciate this mark of confidence

I look forward to pleasant personal relations in the future

I regret exceedingly to inform you

I remain, my dear sir, yours faithfully

I shall be pleased to forward descriptive circulars

I shall esteem it a personal favor

I should welcome an interview at your convenience

I sincerely hope that you will give the subject your earnest consideration

I take pleasure in replying to your inquiry concerning

I trust I shall hear from you soon

I want to express the hope that our pleasant business relations will continue

I want to interest you

I want to thank you for your reply

I wish to confirm my letter

If I can be of further service, please address me

If it is not convenient for you

If there is any valid reason why you are unable

If we can be of service to you

If we can help you in any way

If we have not made everything perfectly clear, please let us know

If you accommodate us, the favor will be greatly appreciated

If you are interested, please let us hear from you

If you are thinking about ordering

If you desire, our representative will call

If you have any cause for dissatisfaction

If you give this matter your prompt attention

In accordance with the terms of our offer

In accordance with your request

In answering your inquiry regarding

In any event, a reply to this will be very much appreciated

In closing we can only assure you

In compliance with your favor

In compliance with your request, we are pleased to send to you

In conclusion, we can assure you

In order to facilitate our future transactions

In reference to your application

In regard to your proposition

In reply thereto, we wish to inform you

In reply to your valued favor

In response to your recent request

In spite of our best efforts it is not probable

In thanking you for the patronage with which you have favored us

In view of all these facts, we feel justified in claiming

Information has just reached me

It gives us pleasure to recommend

It has consistently been our aim to help our customers

It is a matter of great regret to us

It is a pleasure for me to answer your inquiry

It is a well known fact

It is interesting to note

It is our very great pleasure to advise you

It is the policy of our house

It seems clear that our letter must have miscarried

It was purely an oversight on our part

It will be entirely satisfactory to us

It will be our aim to interest you

It will be readily appreciated

It will be to your advantage

It will doubtless be more convenient for you

It will interest you to know

It will receive the same careful attention

Just mail the enclosed card

K

Kindly endorse your reply on the enclosed sheet

Kindly let us have your confirmation at your earliest convenience

Kindly let us know your pleasure concerning

Kindly read the enclosed list

L

Let me thank you for the opportunity to give this matter my personal attention

Let us assure you of our desire to cooperate with you

Let us assure you that we are very much pleased

Let us know if there is any further attention

Let us thank you again for opening an account with us

Looking forward to the early receipt of some of your orders

M

May I ask you to do us a great favor by

May we be favored with a reply

Meantime soliciting your forbearance

Meanwhile permit me to thank you for your kind attention

On referring to your account we notice

Our letter must have gone astray

Our relations with your house must have hitherto been very pleasant

Our services are at your command

Our stock has been temporarily exhausted

Owing to our inability to collect out-standing debts

Permit me to add

Permit us to express our sincere appreciation

Please accept the thanks of the writer

Please consider this letter an acknowledgment

Please favor us with a personal communication

Please feel assured that we shall use every endeavor

Possibly the enclosure may suggest to you

Promptly on receipt of your telegram

Pursuant to your letter

Recently we had occasion

Referring to your esteemed favor

Regretting our inability to serve you in the present instance

Reluctant as we are to believe

Requesting your kind attention to this matter

Should you decide to act upon this latter suggestion

So many requests of a similar nature come to us

Soliciting a continuance of your patronage

T

Thank you for your expression of confidence

Thanking you for your inquiry

Thanking you for your past patronage

Thanking you for your promptness.

Thanking you in advance for an early reply

Thanking you in anticipation

The causes for the delay were beyond our control

The margin of profit which we allow ourselves

The proof is in this fact

The proposition appeals to us as a good one

Therefore we are able to make you this offer

Therefore we trust you will write to us promptly

These points should be most carefully considered

This arrangement will help us over the present difficulty

This is according to our discussion

This matter has been considered very seriously

This personal guarantee I look upon as a service to you

This privileged communication is for the exclusive use

This will amply repay you

Trusting that we may have the pleasure of serving you

Trusting to receive your best consideration

Under no circumstances can we entertain such an arrangement

Under separate cover we are mailing to you

Under these circumstances we are willing to extend the terms

Unfortunately we are compelled at certain times

Unless you can give us reasonable assurance

Upon being advised that these terms are satisfactory

Upon receiving your letter of

We acknowledge with pleasure the receipt of your order

We admit that you are justified in your complaint

We again solicit an opportunity

We again thank you for your inquiry

We always endeavor to please

We appreciate the order you were kind enough to send to us

We appreciate your patronage very much

We are always glad to furnish information

We are anxious to make satisfactory adjustment

We are at a loss to understand why

We are at your service at all times

We are confident that you will have no further trouble

We are extremely desirous of pleasing our patrons

We are in a position to give you considerable help

We are in receipt of your communication regarding

We are indeed sorry to learn

We are perfectly willing to make concessions

We are pleased to receive your request for information

We are pleased to send you descriptive circulars

We are reluctant to adopt such severe measures

We are satisfied regarding your statement

We are sending to you by mail

We are sorry to learn from your letter

We are thoroughly convinced of the need

We are totally at a loss to understand

We are very anxious to have you try

We are very glad to testify to the merit of

We ask for a continuance of your confidence

We ask that you kindly let us hear from you

We assume that you are considering

We assure you of our confidence in the reliability

We assure you of our desire to be of service

We await an early, and we trust, a favorable reply

We await the courtesy of an early answer

We beg a moment of your attention and serious consideration

We believe that if you will carefully consider the matter

We believe you will readily understand our position

We can assure you that any order with which you favor us

We desire information pertaining to your financial condition

We desire to effect a settlement

We desire to express our appreciation of your patronage

We desire to impress upon you

We expect to be in the market soon

We feel assured that you will appreciate

We feel sure that you will approve of our action in this matter

We frankly apologize to you

We hasten to acknowledge the receipt

We have anticipated a heavy demand

We have, as yet, no definite understanding

We have come to the conclusion

We have endeavored to serve the needs of your organization

We have found it impossible

We have much pleasure in answering your inquiry

We have no desire to adopt harsh measures

We have not had the pleasure of placing your name on our ledgers

We have not, however, had the pleasure of hearing from you

We have not yet had time to sift the matter thoroughly

We have the honor to be, gentlemen

We have the honor to inform you

We have thought it best to forward

We have your request for information regarding

We hesitated for a while to pursue the matter

We hope that an understanding can be reached

We hope that we shall have many opportunities to demonstrate our ability

We hope that you will find the enclosed booklet very interesting

We hope to hear favorably from you

We hope you will appreciate

We hope you will excuse the unavoidable delay

We invite your attention to

We must insist upon a prompt settlement

We must, therefore, insist on the terms of the agreement

We note that the time is at hand

We offer you the services of an expert

We particularly want to interest you

We realize that this matter has escaped your attention

We realize that this is simply an oversight on your part

We regret exceedingly that you have been inconvenienced

We regret our inability to meet your wishes

We regret that owing to the press of business

We regret that this misunderstanding has occurred

We regret that we are not in a position

We regret that we are unable to grant your request

We regret the necessity of calling your attention

We regret to be compelled for this reason to withdraw the privilege

We regret to learn that you are disappointed

We remain, dear sir, yours faithfully

We remain, gentlemen, with thanks

We shall await your early commands with interest

We shall await your reply with interest

We shall be glad to fill your order

We shall be glad to have you tell us frankly

We shall be glad to render you any assistance in our power

We shall be happy to meet your requirements

We shall be indebted to you for your courtesy

We shall be pleased to receive the remittance

We shall be pleased to take the matter up further

We shall do everything in our power

We shall do our best to correct the mistake

We shall feel compelled

We shall heartily appreciate any information

We shall use every endeavor

We suggest that this is an opportune time

We suggest that you consider

We take pleasure in enclosing herewith

We take pleasure in explaining the matter you asked about

We take the liberty of deviating from your instructions

We take the liberty of writing to you.

We thank you for calling our attention

We thank you for your courteous letter

We thank you for your kind inquiry of recent date

We thank you very gratefully for your polite and friendly letter

We thank you very much for the frank statement of your affairs

We thank you very sincerely for your assistance

We think you will agree

We trust our explanation will meet with your approval

We trust that we may hear favorably from you

We trust that you will give this matter your immediate attention

We trust you may secure some of the exceptional values

We trust you will find it correct

We trust you will not consider us unduly strict

We trust you will promptly comply with our previous suggestions

We understand your position

We urge that you write to us by early mail

We venture to enclose herewith

We very much wish you to examine

We want every opportunity to demonstrate our willingness

We want particularly to impress upon you this fact

We want to please you in every respect

We want to remind you again

We want you to read the booklet carefully

We will at once enter your order

We will be compelled to take the necessary steps

We will be glad to lay before you the fullest details

We will be pleased to give it careful consideration

We will gladly accommodate you

We will gladly extend to you similar courtesies whenever we can do so

We will make it a point to give your correspondence close attention

We would appreciate a remittance

We would consider it a great favor

We would draw your attention to the fact

We would request, as a special favor

We write to suggest to you

We write to urge upon you the necessity

We wrote to you at length

While we appreciate the peculiar circumstances

While we feel that we are in no way responsible

Why not allow us this opportunity to satisfy you

Will you give us, in confidence, your opinion

Will you give us the benefit of your experience

Will you kindly advise us in order that we may adjust our records

Will you please give us your immediate attention

With our best respects and hoping to hear from you

With reference to your favor of yesterday

With regard to your inquiry

With the fullest assurance that we are considering

With the greatest esteem and respect

You are certainly justified in complaining

You are evidently aware that there is a growing demand

You are quite right in your statement

You cannot regret more than I the necessity

You undoubtedly are aware

You will find interest, we believe, in this advance announcement

You will get the benefit of this liberal offer

You will have particular interest in the new and attractive policy

Your early attention to this matter will oblige

Your further orders will be esteemed

Your inquiry has just been received, and we are glad to send to you

Your orders and commands will always have our prompt and best attention

Your satisfaction will dictate our course

Your trial order is respectfully solicited

Your usual attention will oblige

www.ingramcontent.com/pod-product-compliance
Lightning Source LLC
Chambersburg PA
CBHW071835200526
45169CB00018B/1536